The Concupiscent Mistress

Michelle Hennessy

Made with ❤ on the BookLeaf Publishing Platform
www.bookleafpub.in
www.bookleafpub.com

Dedication

For My Beloved One

Preface

These are simple musings of a girl awakening into her own womanhood. Becoming yourself requires not only shedding old skins but releasing inhibitions. And with that, you can (for me, finally,) embrace the fullness of your sexuality. This is desire in its raw, pure, intense, and powerful state. This is lust built from love. This is the becoming of a Princess.

Acknowledgements

To the love of my life: you inspire everything in me. I am fully me with you, because of you. You see me, and I become. I grow. I thrive. You are my whole heart. Thank you for choosing me, for seeing me, for loving me. This is all for and because of you.

1. Watching Me

Your eyes
Burn a hole through
The back of my skull.
I feel your gaze.
Intense.
No need for me
To turn around.
I know
You're locked into me.
And here I stand,
Frozen in space.
Paralyzed.
By desire.

2. One Look

I never need
To search the crowd for you.
My eyes can find you
In a heartbeat.
I sense you
In the most primal way.
My body can feel your heat;
My ears can hear your heartbeat;
My nose can smell your essence.
Even from hundreds of feet away.
I know you feel me
In the same way.
Our gazes meet,
Locked onto one another.
Never before
Have I been so consumed,
So ravaged,
So ablaze.
It's as though
You fucked me

To my deepest self
With a single glance.

3. On Fire

I feel you.
Close.
Your breath
On my nape,
Taking in my scent.
Do you realize
How weak this makes me?
Do you sense
My body trembling
And on fire?
Do you know
The magic you work within me?
One single touch
And I fear I will crumble
Into embers on the floor.
But I'm willing to take the risk.

4. What if?

What if
Our hands intertwined,
Our eyes locked,
Our breath synchronized?
Would our bodies succumb
Immediately?
Would we pause
And soak it in?
Would our hands
Begin grasping with need?
Would our mouths
Devour one another?
What if
We let it all happen,
Fast and slow,
Taking it in
And hungrily rushing
What if
We have it all?

5. Obsession

I try
All day long
To distract myself,
But I cannot seem to.
My brain floods
With thoughts of you.
I find myself imagining you
Pulling off my clothing.
Methodically,
Piece by piece.
Your hands
Memorizing my body
As you do.
Your mouth
Tracing every part.
My body
Trembling at the command of yours.
My mouth seeking you
With feral hunger.
Our bodies

Melding together
Until we no longer know
Where you end
And I begin.
These thoughts
Leave me on fire.
I burn for you.
I ache for you.
I yearn for you.
I am possessed by you.

6. Fuck

Fuck.
This is bad.
Fuck.
This is good.
This volcanic eruption
I feel inside...
Everything swirls and spins.
Everything is trembling.
Everything is wrong.
Everything is right.
Everything is just...
Fuck.

7. Need

Warm
Your breath on my skin.
I feel you
Searching me
With all of your senses.
The magnetism
Of your raw desire
Pulls me in
Closer to you,
As though I'm a puppet on a string.
Take your hands,
Mold and manipulate me
To feed your every whim and desire.
My need for you is strong.
My need to please you, stronger.
I'm trembling
With anticipation.
Please.
Don't make me wait any longer.

8. An Exhalation

You walk up to me
In what feels like
Slow motion.
I know that
You just want to talk.
But fuck.
As you stand next to me,
All I can focus on
Is the warm air
Coming from your mouth.
Igniting my body
And sending shivers
Down my spine
All at once.
It is intoxicating.
I want to bask
In this heat.
I want to
Envelop myself in it.
Instead,

All I can do
Is say
"Pardon me,
I missed what you said."

9. A Single Breath

Inhaling
Long.
Deep.
Slow.
Taking in
All of my scent.
Your nose
Sketching the line
Of my neck
As if you're
Charting a path
Down my body.
Then
The out-breath.
Warm.
Heavy.
Deliberate.
I hear a soft moan
And I know not
If it escaped my lips

Or yours.
It does not matter.
I can feel
We both want this
As we breathe desire
Into one another.

10. The Pause

We match
The rhythm of our breath.
My exhale
Breathes life into you
And yours
Invigorates me.
Our eyes
Are locked onto each other.
My hand
Softly grazes your cheek,
Finding its way
To your nape
As yours
Firmly grasps my waist,
Pulling me closer to you.
Your lips
Hover over mine.
My heart
Is racing.
Pounding in my ears.

I've waited for this.
I've yearned for this.
And somehow
I ache even more
In this instant.
This moment
Feels like eternity.
Just kiss me.

11. Famished

Your lips.
Soft.
Then,
All at once,
Hungry.
Feeding
On my cheeks,
My neck.
Making their way
To my mouth.
Your tongue
Parts my lips
Like the Red Sea.
I feel you
Seeking the contours
Of my jaw,
Mapping this territory,
Claiming it for yourself.
I sense
My mouth,

Matching your appetite,
Doing its own searching.
I feel as though
I've been starving,
And this union
Has me even more ravenous
For you.
I want
To taste you
Forever.

12. Hands

Your hand
Crawls up my thigh.
I try to reach for yours,
But you grip my hands.
Stopping them.
Shaking your head "no."
"Not yet,"
You whisper
With a slight growl.
Your fingertips
Continue their journey
Upward.
Inward.
My breaths
Become pants.
Gasps.
Moans.
I no longer remember
What I had been seeking
Just moments ago.

All I know is this.
This trembling,
Shaking,
Earth-shattering
Pleasure.
I hear myself
Let out a scream,
And I see you grin,
With a sparkle
In your eyes.
"That's a good girl,"
You say.
And I remember my want.
This time, you nod.
Now, I can have my way
With you.

13. Incendiary

Your face
Buried in my neck.
The warm air
From your breath
Stokes my own inner fire.
I throw my head back
In response to your
Soft groans
In my ear.
Slowly grinding my hips
In your lap.
Moans escape
My mouth.
My nails
Dig into your neck
As your teeth
Clamp into mine.
I am eager
For you.
This passion

Is combustible.
Explosive.
Let's erupt.

14. My Favorite Thing

Kneeling
At your feet.
Looking up at you
With expectant,
Hopeful,
Excited eyes.
You bite your lip
As you undo your pants.
I see that
You are as ready for me
As I am for you.
I let
The length of you
Slide between my fingers,
Admiring you
With my touch.
Then
I slowly run my tongue
From the base to the tip.
"Oh fuck"

You murmur
As I take you in fully,
Swallowing the whole of you.
I'll take you
Slowly.
Firmly.
Your groans.
Writhing.
Deep breaths.
It all
Brings a smile
To my face.
I feel you clench,
Hear you moan.
I continue
To savor you,
Caressing you
With my mouth.
Taking my time.
And then,
I finally taste
Your sweet nectar.
Pleasing you
Pleases me.

15. Biting

I know
You're behind me.
I feel your presence.
Your breath
Hot on my skin.
Your eyes
Boring into my skull.
I feel
Vulnerable.
Self conscious.
As I slowly
Undress
Before you.
"You're so beautiful"
You growl in my ear.
I instinctively lean
My head back into yours
And before I can respond,
I feel your teeth
Sink into my neck

As your grip
Tightens around my arms,
Pulling me more into you.
I gasp
With excitement.
With delight.
"You like that?"
You slyly ask.
I nod,
Unable to speak.
Your nails rip down my arms
And then turn me around.
Aggressive kisses.
You are literally
Devouring me.
And I can't get enough.

16. My Crown

Animalistic.
That's how it feels.
Urgent.
That's how the need is.
Rough.
That's how I want it.
We begin
Tearing at one another.
Clothes scattered and strewn
In a stormy haze.
Hands.
Mouths.
Bodies.
Sweat.
Everything feels like a blur.
I'm not sure how
We ended up on the bed.
But here we are.
You
Behind me.

And I,
I'm ready to be taken.
Your fist
Grasps my hair
At the top of my head.
"This,"
You say
In a commanding voice,
"This is a crown.
A crown for a Princess."
And I wear my crown
As you worship me.
Your Princess.

17. Yummy

Do you
Want a taste?
My lips,
Candy.
My mouth,
Juicy.
Sugar-rimmed skin,
Coated in a glaze
Of sweet sweat.
My body,
Syrupy.
The curve
Of my hip,
A delectable pastry.
My inner thigh,
Ripe.
Luscious.
Begging for a bite.
And between my legs.
Honey.

Dripping.
Precipitated
By the presence
Of you.
Inviting you
To drink it all up.
I see you.
Ravenous.
And I,
A buffet of Eden.
Would you like
To start
With dessert?

18. Rope

Our breaths
Syncopated.
I am kneeling.
Waiting.
Vulnerable.
And trusting.
The soft fibers
Begin to envelop
My torso,
Hugging my arms
Closer to my chest.
"Is this OK?"
You ask me gently.
I nod
As you continue
The bind.
I feel so
Connected to you.
This pattern
Becomes a dance.

The beating of our hearts,
The rhythm.
Our respiration,
The melody.
I melt
Into surrender.
A gasp
Escapes me
As I feel the final knot.
I am fully restrained
And yet somehow
Completely liberated.
I begin to think that
I cannot feel
Any more exhilarated.
Then I feel
Your hands gliding
Up and down my body.
Admiring your art.
"Such a pretty Princess,"
You mutter.
I, a pretty present.
All wrapped up
For you.

19. Stripes

My hands
Press into the wall.
I feel my body trembling.
Anticipating.
Excited.
Wanting.
You trace
My silhouette
With the soft leather.
My breath
Deepens.
"Yes.
Breathe Princess,"
You command.
I feel the gust
From you driving back
With the flogger.
Firmly,
With a sting,
It kisses my skin.

Again.
Again.
I arch
Into every stroke.
My skin
Inflamed.
The ache
Between my thighs
Even more so.
You pause
Massage my skin
With gentle hands
And soft kisses.
My hands
Pull you closer.
"I want more,"
I softly whisper
Into your ear.
I hear you growl
With satisfaction
As I reposition myself.
The bite
Of a new lash
Brushes my exterior.
I deeply moan
Into every strike.
My body

Dancing to this rhythm
You have set.
I sense you
Eclipsing my body
With yours
From behind me.
Both of us
Breathless.
I feel your fingers
Tracing my marks.
Beginning to claw at my skin.
You roar at me
As you throw me
Onto the bed.
I return the growl.
My desire for you
Is as primitive
As your carnal need
For me.
The time has come
To satisfy
This urgent hunger.

20. Suspension

Adorned
In bondage.
Spinning.
On display.
I am
An exhibition.
Solely
For you.
Yours to marvel.
Yours to touch.
Yours to flog.
Yours to savor.
To myself,
I am immovable.
I am only maneuvered
By you.
Molded
By you.
Seen
By you.

Admired
By you.
Released
By you.
Held
By you.
I am
The sole piece.
Designed.
Framed.
Pinned.
In your art gallery.

21. Mine

I lay

In the crook

Of your arm.

Both of us

Panting for breath.

Drenched.

Your fingers

Intertwined

With my own.

You still

Nibble at my neck.

As I hum

Gentle moans

And arch into you.

Melding myself

More with you.

My free hand

Claws into your neck.

Gripping you tightly

With a fear

Of you pulling away.
You respond
With a soft,
Reassuring murmur,
"I love you, Princess.
I'm keeping you.
You're mine."
This whisper
Sends chills
Down my body.
This is surrender.
This is submission.
This is trust.
This is safety.
This is love.
"I love you, too,"
I answer.
"I am yours.
Forever."
You pull me to you
And with a thunder
That comes from within,
You lightly growl
In my ear.
"Mine."
Yes, Beloved.
I am yours.